HOUSES

THE ARCHITECTURE OF
NAGLE HARTRAY
DANKER KAGAN
MCKAY PENNEY

First published in the United States of America by Edizioni Press, Inc. 469 West 21st Street New York, New York 10011 www.edizionipress.com

ISBN: 1-931536-44-9

Library of Congress Catalogue Card Number: 2005927265 Printed in China

Design:
Gary Kon
Editor:
Sarah Palmer
Editorial Assistant:
Nancy Sul

The Hybridization of Midwestern Modernism

It is generally understood that 20th-century modern architecture, like its antecedent formalistically driven Western styles, emanated first in the Middle East, and then later in Europe. Historically, American architecture—domestic and otherwise—on the other hand, is understood to be a hybridization of earlier forms. Perhaps this comes about as a natural result of this country's innate cultural multivalent condition in which there are few, if any, "originals" present. With the possible exception of Native Americans, the United States is a land of émigrés and exiles, whereas in Europe originals abound (1).

The 31 (2) domestic works shown here are no exception to the broadest definition of hybridization (3). They are composed predominantly of mutations on the theme of the purebred—thus the hybrid. Certainly, the initial section of this book—the 15 so-called "Classics" houses—are the ones closest to their European progenitors (4) (even devoid of the presence of so much as a single visible roof). On the other hand, the six "Pops" houses in the second section are predominantly protected by the presence of roofs, and a far greater use of naturally expressed materials—a kind of "below-the-salt" vernacular, somewhat less detached from the land than the houses of the first group. The final ten (as it were) "Jazz" houses are derived generally from more complex programs resulting in linked pavilions, each of which has a substantial attachment to the land (5). The aggregation of the whole is not so much a product of an evolving theme as it is the particularized use of an emerging palette-in-the-process-of-becoming.

Irrespective of Jim Nagle's architectural education (6) that was so indebted to European precedent, his Midwest birthplace combined with virtually four decades of professional practice in Chicago situate him squarely within an architectural tradition that relates more naturally to the American prairie than to European antecedents (7). While Frank Lloyd Wright had a unique vision for a so-called "organic" American architecture, there are precious few Wrightian acolytes at work in America today. Wright's architectural production was simply too complex either for replication or hybridization. Not so for Mies van der Rohe and his lowland colleagues. Modernism was, in any case, itself a European hybridization of Wright's seminal 1910 German exhibition and publication (8), consciously and reductively misperceiving precedent toward an end that European architects found particularly useful in an otherwise revolutionary epoch.

When modernist architecture landed back on the American continent from whence it had emanated as a result of WWII, it was one of the happy accidents of the 20th century for young American architects. In any case, Americans were used to pragmatically transforming arcane ideas into useful realities. This was simply one more (architectural) challenge—but one that had originated in the United States, and had (perhaps presciently) returned home.

The work of Nagle and his associates represents a kind of normative, clearly American architectural production that is as grounded in the making of things as it is in a formal understanding of Western traditions. As such it is a kind of amalgam that is well understood within the Chicago architectural tradition, hybridized as they (and we) are. By that I mean that, whereas Eastern architects owe a debt to Le Corbusier and Louis Kahn (i.e. in the sense of the absence of detail—indeed in the absence of "material" while formalist in inclination), Chicago architecture (because of both Wright and Mies) is solidly grounded within the presence of detailing material substance. Nagle's formal antecedents are certainly indebted to Le Corbusier, while his constructional antecedents look to Wright and to Mies for inspiration.

As well as many other American architects who were products of an architectural education grounded in and informed by modernism, Nagle and later his colleagues—who, with the single exception of Jack Hartray, grew from within the firm—understood the appropriateness of an architecture well-suited to the American prairie. Their domestic work shown here is as uncluttered as any coming out of the last quarter of the 20th century. Not only as exemplary of its type and its time from a relative point of view, but utterly unto itself, Nagle—and now his partner/descendants—are positioned well within the Midwest tradition of well-crafted, thorough, capable production. It is entirely fitting to see that tradition alive and well in Chicago.

1. Simplistically, one finds Frenchmen in France, Germans in Germany, Italians in Italy, whereas in the United States, multiple populations exist interdependently (if, sometimes uneasily). It follows that French (German, Italian, etc.) architecture is particularized to its population and simultaneously informed by its long history, whereas American architecture is an amalgam of its many etymological origins, with only its recent history to inform it—thus it is hybridized. 2. For purposes of modernist clarity, the architects have excluded houses they have authored that are more historically inclined. 3. While each of the three book divisions ends with two commercial/institutional examples (to suggest a logical transition to more substantial structures), it is Jim Nagle's single-family houses that inform the entire publication, and, as such, warrant scrutiny. In any case, the domestic work constitutes the vast majority of the work in this document. 4. It is no accident that Nagle spent several periods of time in Europe (primarily Holland) early in his career absorbing the modernist architecture of Le Corbusier, Mies van der Rohe, Oud, Rietveld, etc. 5. These final ten, rather more complex structures, pave the way for Nagle and his collaborators to shift focus to larger scale, non-domestic architectural production. 6. Stanford, MIT, Harvard. 7. I should say that Jim Nagle was in my employ from 1965 to 1966, immediately after which he began his architectural practice as a partnership with Larry Booth. 8. The Wasmuth publication (documenting the seminal Berlin exhibition of Wright's work) was acknowledged by Europe's leading modernist proponents to have been a powerful influence, first on their architectural perceptions, later on their architectural production.

Stanley Tigerman
Chicago, 2005

Classics, Pops & Jazz

It is difficult to sum up a body of architectural work, especially when the work spans nearly 40 years and a paradigmatic shift and re-shift in architectural thought regarding the relationship between design and its physical and historical context. One tends to look for constants in order to create a linear progression in which the design of each building builds upon and improves the ideas inherent in the previous work. In examining our own work, we have found that the constants are not so much related to the form or style of the buildings as they are to our attitude and approach to the complexities of a given problem. This is particularly true of our houses.

A strong undercurrent of Modernism unites all of these seemingly individual works. This is evident in the attention to materiality and construction, and our concern for volume and space over surface. But it is a Modernism humanized. The human element is dominant in all of our work, especially in the houses, and it is our responsiveness to the particularities of each context that leads to diverse designs despite the underlying consistency. Even in the earliest and most "modern" houses, the purity of the formal idea adapts to its site, context, and program, and incorporates careful attention to scale. Our work has always examined the relationships between interior and exterior spaces and integrates these spaces into the way the individual or family functions.

Our approach to the design of each house is often influenced by the relative restrictiveness of the site or the particular desires of the client. The houses tend to arrange themselves into three types, which

we often describe in terms of a musical analogy. The musical styles of "Classics, Pops, and Jazz" loosely describe our pluralistic approach, in terms of both form and attitude. The "classic" Modern house usually occupies a restricted site with little room for formal maneuvering. It tends to be an object-building in either the landscape or cityscape, with an easily defined volume. It has a clear formal parti and structure, and a formal spatial organization. Its roots are Miesian, but softened through material and detail.

A specific desire on the part of a client or a compelling feature of a site may suggest a second approach, which, like popular music, borrows from vernacular culture. Typically these are country houses, built with natural materials such as wood and stone, which take their cues from the topography and local structures. Through either their form or material, these houses suggest interpretations of vernacular buildings. Upon examination, however, details such as flush corners, sunscreens, and the abstract treatment of the material are entirely modern in sensibility. In many of these houses the vernacular first impression thinly disguises the same spatial and material issues present in all our work.

Finally, on a less restricted site, the ability to create more fluid compositions leads to more informal and asymmetrical compositions. With its syncopated rhythms of vertical and horizontal spatial sequences, the "jazz" house is more intuitively than formally driven. It relies on the experience of rhythm and movement through space, rather than on a formal parti. Repetition of windows, sunscreens, and other tectonic devices reinforce the sense of movement, while the abstract handling of material integrates the themes and unifies the composition.

classics

Translucens House Dallas, Texas (1999-2004)

Previous clients decided to build a new house on a 75- by 225- foot lot closer to downtown Dallas and better suited to their new lives with children and grandchildren as visitors. The house is set back from the street and wrapped around a courtyard with a lap pool. Art is displayed throughout the spaces but especially in the 24- by 60-foot living room. With garages and service areas off the alley, the kitchen and dining area is at the rear while bedrooms and offices areas are at the front. The upper floor has glass bridge connections over the entry and above the courtyard to access the rooftop sculpture garden. The steps at the entry also bridge a water flow over a black granite base, which wraps the floating floor. The basement is primarily a gallery for the display of a doll collection. A theater, workroom, and storage area are also housed here.

White-painted steel frame construction with white aluminum wall panels and various glass types and connection details form the minimalist composition. This "Translucens House" uses glass to blur the exterior and interior bounderies.

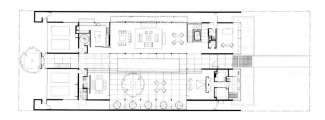

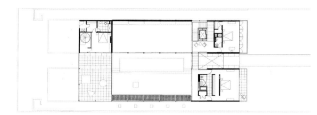

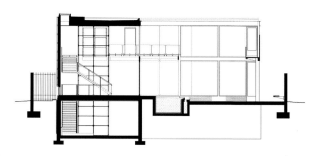

16   Translucens House

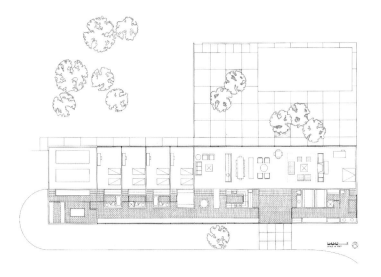

20 Dallas House

Dallas House

Dallas, Texas (1972-73) This long, low house was designed to form a comfortable and restrained backdrop for views and for the clients' collection of modern painting, sculpture, and furniture. The 150-foot-long white stucco house with dark window frames is an abstract composition of minimalist forms. The north portion of the house, through which one enters, has eight-foot ceilings and houses services and a linear gallery space. From this space, one steps 30 inches down to the living and sleeping spaces, which overlook the pool and view. Mexican travertine and dark stained oak floors contrast with white plaster floors and ceilings. The house is a simple, controlled, but uplifting and spacious environment.

Architect's Cottage

Door County, Wisconsin

(1997-99) This three-acre site is 230 feet of beach frontage on Lake Michigan with an existing small cabin dating from 1946, which the owner/architect used as a family getaway for 25 years. The children and their families took over the cabin and the architect built a new 1,500-square-foot pavilion plus porches. In building the cottage, the architect wanted to maximize views to the lake and woods with as little impact on the natural environment and neighboring cottages as possible. The required beach set-back allowed the one-story structure to parallel the first dune and use the hill of the second dune as a buffer. The approach path follows the dune contours around to the entry porch at the center of the structure.

The wood frame pavilion is clad with natural finish clear cedar siding. Clerestory windows, which surround the front and side of the structure as well as the 12-foot-wide rolling glass doors, are insulated glass with polished mahogany frames. Local fieldstone was used for the fireplace (which anchors the composition), exterior retaining walls, and walkways. The interior nine-foot-high ceilings are clear varnished cedar, floors are clear fir, doors are river birch, cabinets/built-ins are white maple, and most of the furniture is beechwood. White plaster walls work as a backdrop for the natural materials and sparsely placed abstract lithographs.

Located at the north end of the home, the guest room is separated from the living room by a study/den. Bathrooms, utility areas, and the kitchen back up the living quarters, allowing lake views. The basement and crawl space house mechanical equipment, a shop, and storage. A two-way fireplace separates the living/dining area from the master bedroom alcove. The south-facing porch, with a view to the lake, has a wood trellis which filters the sunlight and protects the glass walls. The screened porch at the north end is framed to create an outdoor room. Columns add to the modest monumentality of the building. Existing trees were carefully pruned for privacy and selected views to the bay shore.

The architect and his wife wished for some time to construct a modern cottage which worked both technically and aesthetically. Resolving the building problems of earlier modernism was one goal, and making a statement about modesty, context, environment and space another.

A carport, a beach firepit, and more stone walkways have since been added to the compound.

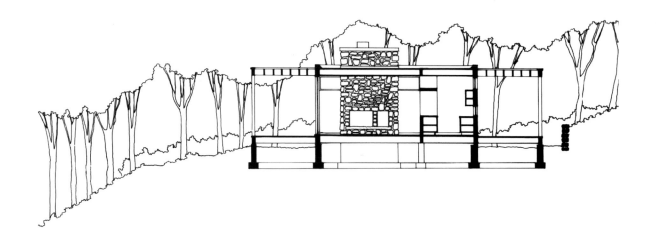

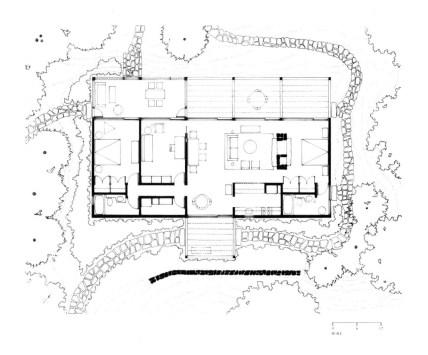

SCALE

26 Architect's Cottage

Carpenter's House

Elmhurst, Illinois (1997-98) Built on an existing 60-foot lot in the post-war suburb of Elmhurst, Illinois, this one-story courtyard house was designed for and built by a contractor/carpenter. The client wanted a simple, elegant environment that provided for expansion in the basement area below the one story L-shaped plan. The focus of the house is toward the rear garden and pool.

The architect thought of the house as a prototype that actually fits into the scale of the neighborhood—and it has been well received. Some of the firm's staff even helped with the framing. The exterior is clear cedar siding with black metal window and door frames that have sun-control devices. Ceilings are nine feet high throughout the interior, with white drywall, dark oak floors, and maple cabinetry and paneling. All classic modern fixtures and furniture were selected with this unusual client.

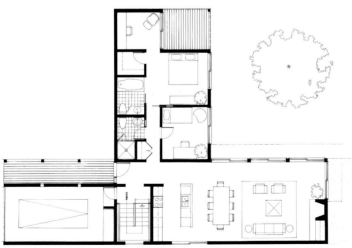

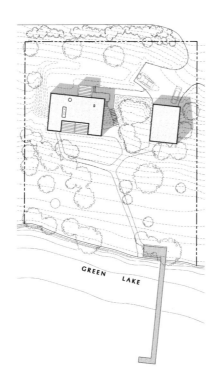

GREEN LAKE

Green Lake Cottage Green Lake, Wisconsin

(2000-03) This second home/retirement cottage follows the contours of an oak-covered hillside over-looking Green Lake, as does a garage/boathouse out-building. The two-story steel and wood framed structure houses an upper level entry (containing living, dining, and master bedroom) and lower level walk out (with children's bedrooms and family area). The garage/boathouse, with lower level kayak storage, aligns with the house, preserving the trees between.

Both house and garage are clad in horizontal clear cedar siding with black framed windows and trim. The downhill elevation is a post and beam frame with alternating screen porches and open decks. Horizontal lattice on the lower concrete will be planted with ivy.

Inside, black slate and hickory floors are used with white plaster walls and clear cedar ceilings. Natural limestone for the fireplaces and exterior walks and retaining walls comes from nearby Wisconsin quarries. Screen porches alternate with open decks on both lakefront floors.

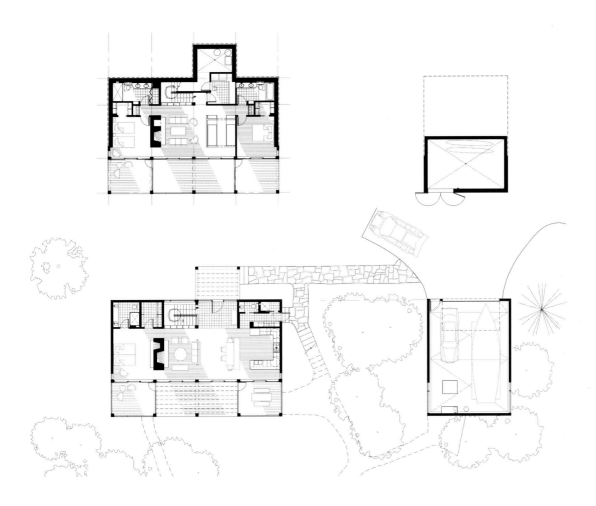

Deerpath House

Door County, Wisconsin (1995-96) The deer path that meanders through this isolated site on the shore of Lake Michigan inspired the bi-nuclear form of the house, which is bisected by the path. It is a classic modern parti, as that found in Marcel Breuer's houses. But in this design, the connecting link is flushed out, so the split is not immediately apparent. The surface of the building reads as continuous, with horizontal flush cedar siding and horizontal mullions forming a taut, unbroken skin. The house is balanced and serene, reflecting the character of its owners.

The house was sited to capture views in a number of directions: to the lake, to the woods, and to the point. The glass entry separates the sleeping wing from the living wing. The flooring here continues the lines of the decks with mahogany strips between the maple floor planks, with the glass suggesting continuity of indoor and outdoor space between the two wings. The house is based upon a seven-foot module both horizontally and vertically so ceilings are seven feet high or double that, and pavilions are 15 by 37 feet. The entry deck and lakeside deck are 22 square feet.

Durkes House

Dixon, Illinois (1977-78) The vertical, compact nature of this house grew from considerations of siting, spatial development, and practicality of construction and budget. The building is an object in the landscape, its footprint barely disturbing a stand of mature trees along the Rock River. The main living spaces begin at the second floor and take advantage of the views, with a two-story living room and porch spaces carved out of the block at either end, and a treetop roof terrace off of the fourth floor study. As desired by the clients, the house has a formal center entry with defined rooms. Yet there is also spatial flow and simplicity of detailing that make the house more modern. Horizontal cedar siding and the stair, which recalls nearby farm silos, add scale and detail to counterbalance the abstract geometry. The owners subsequently moved back to the city and even attempted to move the house with them.

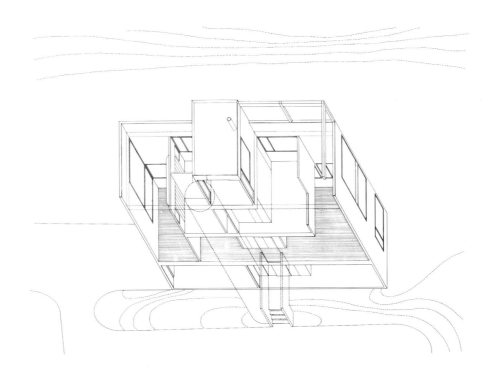

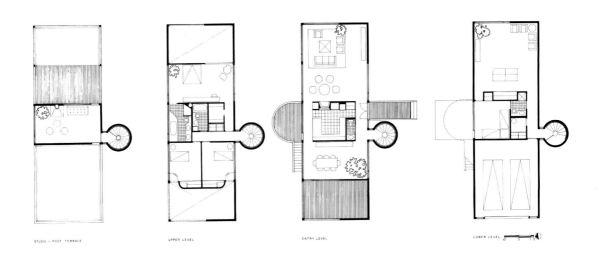

STUDIO - ROOF TERRACE   UPPER LEVEL   ENTRY LEVEL   LOWER LEVEL

Dunes House

South Haven, Michigan (1990-91) A steeply sloping site overlooking Lake Michigan had a limited buildable area. This suggested a compact building form detached from the densely wooded site. The three-story cubic volume rises from the edge of the dune, establishing a clear counterpoint to the natural landscape. As originally designed, the house was placed within a circle inscribed in the landscape. This area outlined the limits of intrusion on the natural world, including the footprints of the pool and garage, and was to have been planted with dune grass. Subsequent siting changes were made in the arrangement of pool and landscaping, but the original intent is intact.

The sculptural composition is subtractive: a large outdoor room is carved out of the cubic volume, the edges of which are defined by the structural frame. The open joist roof helps to screen the strong west sun and the curve of the wall, which separates interior from exterior, forming a counterpoint to the rigid geometry of the enclosure. Interior spaces are arranged on two sides of the exterior room in a roughly L-shaped plan, and all spaces overlook the lake with access to terraces. Entry is at the second level main living floor. Children's bedrooms occupy the first floor while master bedroom and study occupy the third.

The choice and detailing of exterior materials is consistent with the abstract quality of the overall building form, but they also suggest marine construction, inspired by the lakefront site. Stained cedar plywood panels on a varying module are separated by aluminum reveals. Windows work within the construction module for a streamlined feel, varying in size according to the need to either limit or admit sunlight and views. The exterior spiral stair, painted steel railings, and ship's ladder to the roof play up the nautical imagery. The house also recalls Le Corbusier's villas with outdoor rooms.

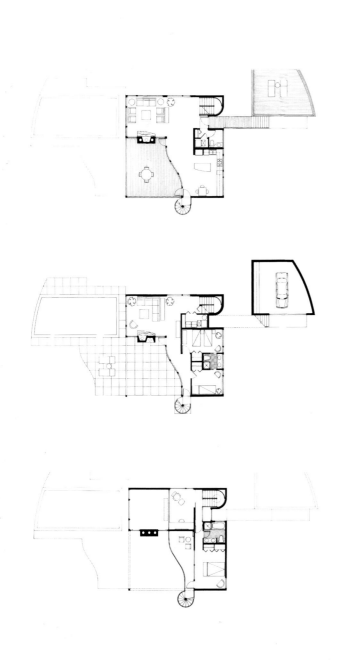

46 Dunes House

Minnesota House

Northern Minnesota (1969-70) The Minnesota House takes the Bauhaus box and adds a 45-degree rotation of the interior and the separate garage for added spatial complexity. The rotation also relates to the site; the house rises dramatically from a sloped point of land projecting into an inland lake. The use of vertical cedar siding introduces traditional materials and scale to an otherwise abstract composition and relates to the vertical rhythm of the pines which grow down to the water's edge. Cold spring granite from a nearby quarry was used for the central fireplace mass, and the exterior granite walls were recycled from the scout camp which was formerly on the site. Variations of five different woods on the interior create a backdrop for the classic modern furniture and detailing. A guest house will be added to the garage roof soon.

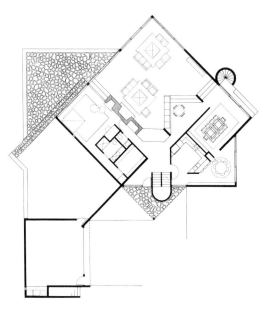

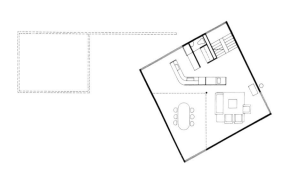

Brown House

Des Moines, Iowa (1969-70) Built at the end of a cul-de-sac street in Des Moines, Iowa, this house overlooks a wooded ravine to the south. The lot had never been built on due to the steep site. By locating the garage near the street and stretching the pedestrian entry along the connecting wall, the four-story-high square plan fit the setbacks. Twisting the plan 22.5 degrees allows for unexpected overlooks. The children's top floor overlooks the upper living/den which in turn overlooks the living/dining area.

The exterior language of the composition is white stucco (Bauhaus), but the subdivision of space is Structurist. Red, yellow, and blue accent panels and walls float within the interior stucco-finished enclosure and oak floor planes. Another house/winery was built for this client.

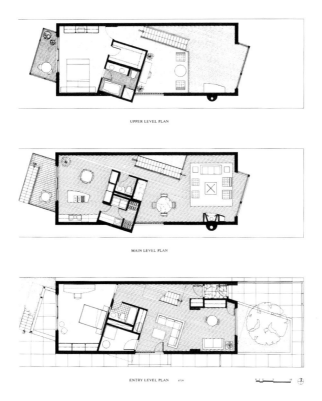

UPPER LEVEL PLAN

MAIN LEVEL PLAN

ENTRY LEVEL PLAN

Lincoln Park House Chicago, Illinois (1988-1989) This

house is a variation on the typical Chicago Victorian townhouse, many of which feature a large window or bay on the street façade. In this case the bay becomes oversized and aligns with a plan grid shift; the shift of core, stair, and front and back bays is used to create more spatial interest and natural light within the narrow lot. A catenary second floor balcony and the large bays accentuate the lightness of the interior. A uniform quality of interior light and a general sense of lightness were particularly important in this project, as the clients have an extensive art collection.

Evanston House

Evanston, Illinois (1973-74) Located just into Evanston, the first suburb north of Chicago, this steel and brick house is on a private street in a dense suburban complex. Issues of privacy suggested the courtyard house parti, a simple ten-foot-high volume open to walled courtyards front and back and reminiscent of Mies van der Rohe's courtyard houses of the 1930s. Spanning from east to west, walls with bar joists allowed for complete freedom to manipulate space with curved walls, and to open up glass elevations to the gardens, eliminating the sense of separation from the outside. Like the Lincoln Park house, space flows around objects in the plan that float free from the orthogonal. The master bedroom quarters to the south and children's rooms to the north shape the family spaces which flow diagonally through the plan and are accentuated by an eight-foot skylight in the center.

Footnote: A summer cottage in Wisconsin was built for this client in 1984.

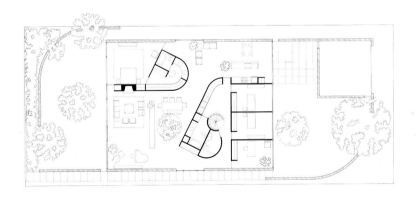

Atrium House
Chicago, Illinois (1987-88) This three-story brick house in a Chicago neighborhood replaced an earlier frame bungalow. The client wanted a studio-like environment with work spaces and living spaces together. The ground floor entry leads to a central atrium stair which is enclosed with glass block walls with skylights above. Steel bridges with glass block floors span the central space and a steel stair connects the bridges vertically. This void divides the house into front and back. The lower office, kitchen/dining area, and upper studio are in the rear, behind the guest room, living room, and master bedroom in the front. The front bay is reinterpreted from the neighborhood with glass block, curved glass, and steel detailing anticipating the interior spaces and finishes.

Hunziker House

Chicago, Illinois (1983-84) Demolished 2002.

This house is typical of the classic modern houses that the architect has designed for dense urban sites, in this case a typical 25-foot-wide Chicago lot. The creation of light and open space governs the design, which also has to recognize its context. On this particular neighborhood street, bungalows, houses, and three-flats provide an eclectic mix of scale and material. The opportunity existed, therefore, to develop a more modern design, while simultaneously responding to the surrounding urban scale. The stucco house with its large offset two-story bay recalls both the asymmetry of the traditional Victorian house and the style of the 1930s Chicago Bauhaus buildings found nearby. It represents a Modernism filtered through 1930s eclecticism which was less abstract in detail. The scale of the details—horizontal stucco joints and the base, curved jambs, glass block, and stone lintels and sills— responds to the scale of detail in the neighborhood.

Unlike the typical Chicago lot, there is no alley at the rear, so the garage is accessed from the street, lifting the main spaces to the floor above. At the rear, a vine-covered trellis echoes the entry bay on the street, and a stair leads from the kitchen to the long garden. The plan is more open than most, reflecting the attitudes of the client as well as the inclination of the architect. Softly sculptured spaces are evenly washed with light introduced through windows, the glass block wall at the stair, and sky-lights. A soft neutral palette of off-white walls and travertine floors emphasizes space over enclosure.

Footnote: This house was purchased from a subsequent owner and demolished by a neighbor who built a large house in the 1990s. The lot is now a sideyard.

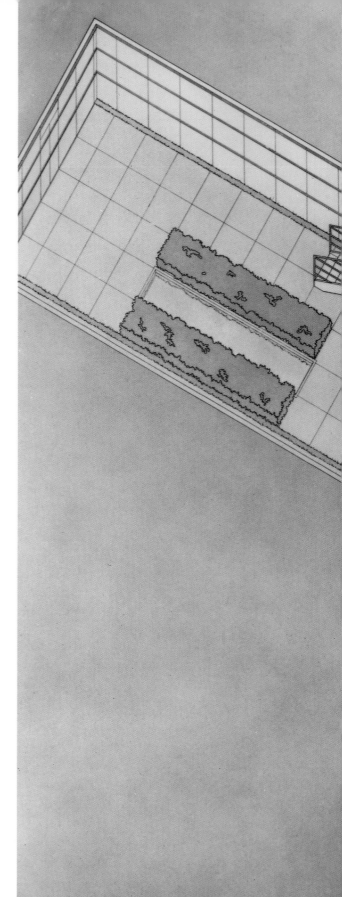

THIRD FLOOR PLAN

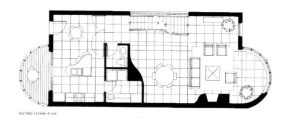

SECOND FLOOR PLAN

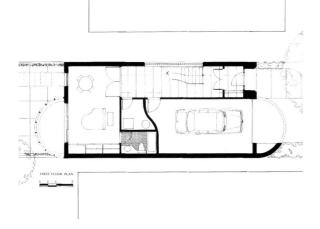

FIRST FLOOR PLAN

66   Hunziker House

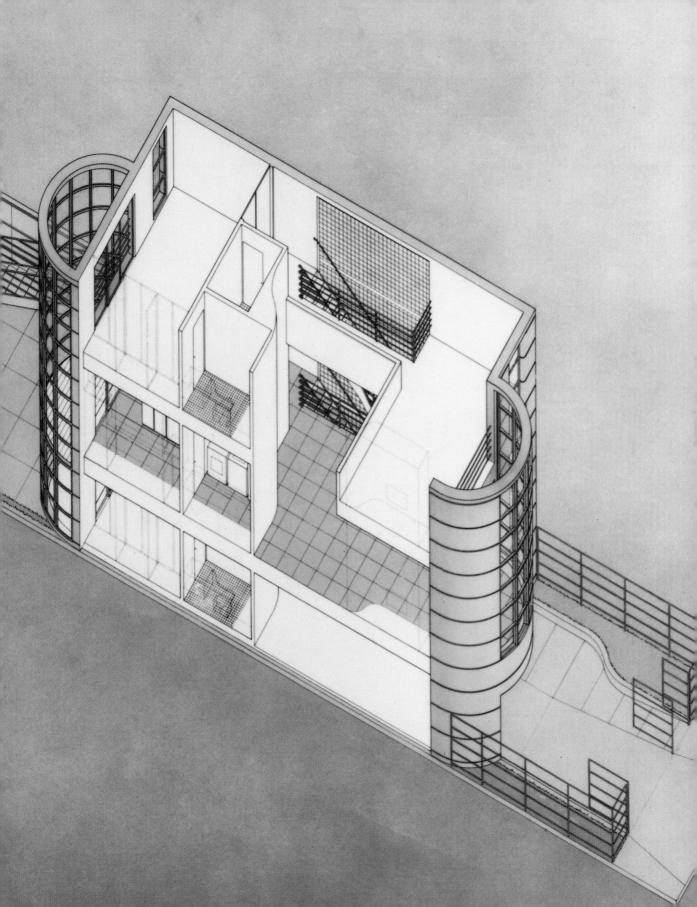

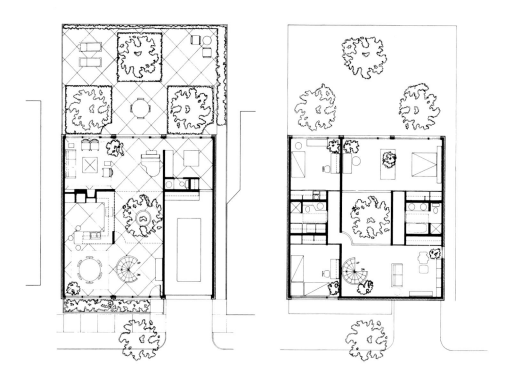

James Nagle House

Chicago, Illinois (1977-78) Built several years earlier than the Hunziker House, the architect's own house explores similar issues of spatial flow around a central vertical void, though with a more abstract language than the later design. Located on an atypically wide lot on a quiet cul-de-sac street in a dense neighborhood, this house is inwardly focused yet responsive to the surrounding context, modern in expression yet scaled to the neighborhood. Large ground floor openings recall the garage doors of nearby coach houses, and the building maintains the same set-back, overall scale, and materials as its neighbors. Organized on a nine-square around a central vertical light-well, the plan allows for spatial openness both vertically and horizontally. The back courtyard garden continues both the 12-foot grid and the terrazzo flooring of the first floor living spaces for uninterrupted flow between interior and exterior living spaces.

Schiller Street Townhouses

Chicago, Illinois (1986-87) A series of five infill townhouses elaborates on the issue of scale, detail, and light explored earlier in the Hunziker House. The houses front a narrow east/west avenue off busy LaSalle Street. The projecting bays are glazed three-quarters around, and oriented to maintain the privacy of each while admitting east light and longer views. This is the clearest project illustrating how single-family design informs larger projects built by the architect.

401 East Ontario
Chicago, Illinois (1987-91) This 52-story tower sited in Chicago's Streeterville neighborhood contains 394 units, commercial space at street level, health and recreational facilities with roof terraces, and five levels of concealed parking at the base. Each unit enjoys at least one large bay window angled to the city and lake views. Corner units have 180-degree exposures. The interior feeling is that of "townhouses in the sky" with classically organized floor plans. The care in design (especially the plans) comes from an understanding of how each house works in a "community."

pops

Lakeside Retreat
Lakeside, Michigan (1970, 1981-82, 1995-96)

The design of this house is grounded in the vernacular building tradition of the Midwest, both in material and concept, though the forms themselves are abstract. This was in part due to the desires of the clients and the history behind the current house. In a way, it refers back to its own history as well as to other buildings.

The site is a long wooded strip that falls off dramatically in a steep bluff overlooking Lake Michigan with views west as far as Chicago. In the early 1970s the architect built a small second house on the site for this family with four small children. A few years later, they built a two-story guesthouse over the edge of the bluff, its roof deck level with the top of the bluff and accessed by a bridge. By the early 1990s, the children had families of their own, and the two small houses were strained. As the clients were very attached to the main house, with its happy associations, the architect first generated several studies for adding onto it or even building a third structure on the property. It became apparent, however, that none of these approaches would solve their desire to create one place where the extended family could come together, and ultimately the decision was made to demolish the original structure and build a new one while adding vertically to the guesthouse.

The old house became the spiritual center of the new, which literally wrapped around it. Where the

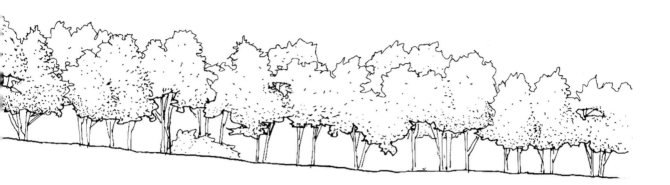

original house once stood is an outdoor circular fire pit made of granite recycled from the old fireplace. There, sheltered from wind by the semicircular form of the new house, the families can congregate and enjoy the west views.

The new house, though very different in form and detail from the original wedge-shaped volume, recalls the old in the use of materials; both the house and guesthouse are clad with vertical clear cedar siding, both have terne metal roofs sloped to the view, and the fireplace of the main house uses the same granite as in the original. That fireplace anchors a two-story living and gathering space. The vernacular quality of the architecture is carried through with exterior cedar sunscreens (reminiscent of boat outriggers) and maple floors, railings, and doors. The semicircular form itself recalls to some degree Frank Lloyd Wright's solar hemicycle houses of the 1940s.

The guesthouse addition was a particularly challenging problem; any alteration had to maintain the original footprint of the house, since new construction over the bluff edge is no longer permitted. The third floor main living area cantilevers over the remodeled space below, all of which was reclad in natural cedar. It is connected to the bluff with a new bridge and appears to hang over the edge of the bluff, floating in the trees. The family nicknamed it the "Tree House" and the main house the "Press Box," names which complement the spirit of the architecture.

LAKESIDE RETREAT, MICHIGAN

FIRST FLOOR PLAN

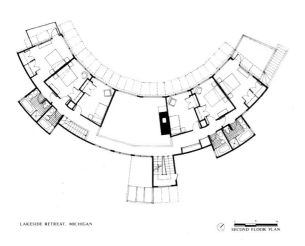

LAKESIDE RETREAT, MICHIGAN

SECOND FLOOR PLAN

80 Lakeside Retreat

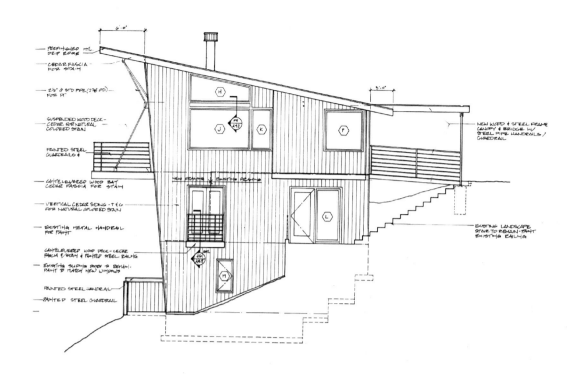

- PREFINISHED MTL DRIP EDGE
- CEDAR FASCIA FOR STAIN
- 2½" Ø STD PIPE (2⅞" OD) FOR PT
- SUSPENDED WOOD DECK - CEDAR FOR NATURAL COLORED STAIN
- PAINTED STEEL GUARDRAILS &
- CANTILEVERED WOOD BAY CEDAR FASCIA FOR STAIN
- VERTICAL CEDAR SIDING - T&G FOR NATURAL COLORED STAIN
- EXISTING METAL HANDRAIL FOR PAINT
- CANTILEVERED WOOD DECK - CEDAR FASCIA F/STAIN & PAINTED STEEL RAILING
- EXISTING SLIDING DOOR TO REMAIN - PAINT TO MATCH NEW WINDOWS
- PAINTED STEEL HANDRAIL
- PAINTED STEEL GUARDRAIL

NEW WOOD & STEEL FRAME CANOPY & BRIDGE W/ STEEL PIPE HANDRAILS / GUARDRAIL

EXISTING LANDSCAPE STAIR TO REMAIN - PAINT EXISTING RAILING

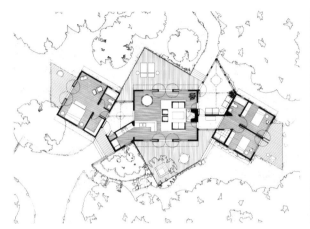 

Hilltop House

Bridgman, Michigan (1988-89) Built for a couple and their grown children, this vacation house was sited on a linear saddle atop a heavily wooded ridge. Personal memories of summer camping were invoked in the design of three interlocking cabins, each with outdoor decks: the parents occupy the westerly cabin and the children and guests the easterly one, while the central cabin is a dining and living area. The residential space created by the fragmentation of the house becomes the entry on the front to the southwest, and the screen porch at the rear (to the northeast) is connected by the flat roof links. Above the entry link, a fifth deck provides a platform for long views into the woods; a ship's mast on the deck serves as a flagpole.

The exterior is all frame construction with standing seam metal roofs, shiplap cedar siding, gray painted window trim, wood sunscreens, and exposed plank decks with metal capped posts and turn buckle cable rails. Inside are wood floors, white plaster walls, wood trim, and exposed trusses. The intermediate spaces have polished concrete floors and exterior siding.

The camp is intended to provide a relaxed environment with privacy, community, nature, and good times in mind.

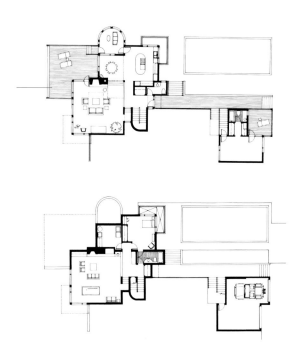

Shingle House

Union Pier, Michigan (1993-95) The Shingle House strikes a balance between the clients' desire for a traditional country cottage and the architect's interest in exploring more complex spatial relationships reminiscent of early 20th century modernism. The result is that, while the overall massing is modern, cedar shingles, white trim, and rounded corners create a continuity of surface and a language that suggests a more traditional imagery.

The narrowness of the lakefront lot led to a compact tubular composition with the guesthouse/garage and pool pulled away from the house along the entry boardwalk. In the main house, seven interlocking vertical volumes of varying heights open to each other internally to form complex spaces in section. Vertical floor openings placed diagonally through the section create changing internal vistas in addition to the lake views, while screen walls and selective placement of openings in the exterior walls screen views of the houses on adjacent lots.

The entry from the connecting deck provides a view through the living area, but one must turn and step down to the space. The connections and views throughout the house continue this subtle complexity. Precedents for these forms relate to the De Stijl investigation of neo-plastic space. The functional requirements of the young growing family are solved while the environment is enhanced by complexity, variation, and particularization.

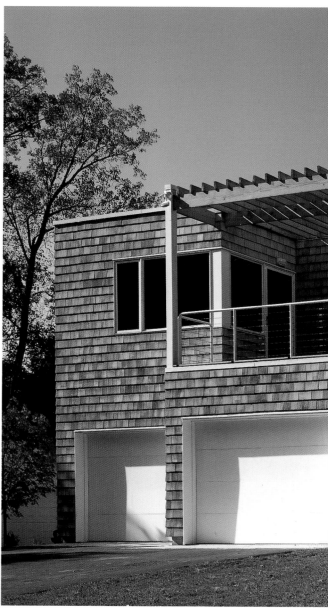

Family Lighthouse
Marshall Point, Wisconsin (1979-81)

This vacation house in Northern Wisconsin is similar to the Shingle House in its vernacular use of natural materials (shingles, vertical siding, stone, and stovewood) and regional recall. But the geometry is simple—a pure octagon—recalling the nearby lighthouses on the peninsula. The interior is a post and beam square with a central staircase connecting bedrooms below to the living space and rooftop observatory. All interior floor, wall, and ceiling surfaces are natural finished fir. Overlooks, lofts, and triangulated spaces provide surprises.

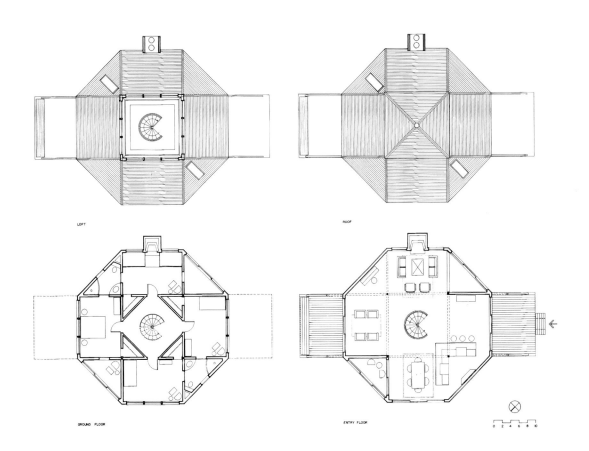

LOFT

ROOF

GROUND FLOOR

ENTRY FLOOR

0 2 4 6 8 10

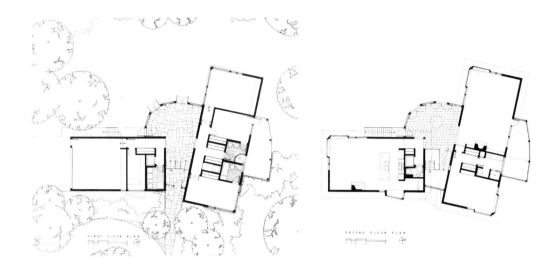

FIRST FLOOR PLAN

SECOND FLOOR PLAN

Lakeside House

Lakeside, Michigan (1993-94) A couple with grown children wanted a special but less abstract house to retire to, with open and comfortable spaces from which to enjoy the peaceful natural setting. The house sits on the edge of an open meadow, once farmland, surrounded by woods. There are views to Lake Michigan, and the woods, ravine, and wildflower meadow. The architect's answer was to create a structure using natural materials in clearly recognizable volumes, but to shift their orientation and detail them in a way that was not formal or traditional.

The house was split into two separate stucco pavilions, each with a curved terne metal roof, and connected by a steel-framed glass link with a mid-level entry. The stucco of the pavilions wraps inside this space, which is floored with tile and is fully glazed to emphasize its interior/exterior ambiguity. The main living spaces on the upper level are open under a ceiling of curved laminated beams and wood decking. The pavilions are oriented toward each other at a slightly splayed angle to suggest a loose, informal attitude and emphasize the entry as the space between two objects. Corner projected "box" windows set up a conversation between the two parts of the house and are an unexpected counterpoint to the simplicity of the exterior, as is the trellis deck with screen porch below. The angles relate directly to the views and form residual landscaped exterior forecourts.

Beach House
Door County, Wisconsin (1998-99) This 2,000-square-foot house is located on a wooded site looking east to Lake Michigan. The original cottage to the north shares driveway access and utilities. The clients are a retired couple with grown children who wanted a permanent home with guest quarters in the original cottage.

The structure is simple frame construction clad in gray stained cedar siding with white trim and stainless steel copings and scuppers. The living room is capped with a raised laminated beam roof which curves out to the lake view. The nautical reference is reinforced with wood floors and trim. The local fieldstone fireplace anchors the space with the den tucked behind. Guest bedroom and master bedrooms are located at opposite ends of the cottage. The screen porch and trellised deck on the lake side of the house provide summer outdoor spaces.

Furnishings, cabinets, and built-ins were locally constructed of maple and beechwood. The natural landscape and fieldstone paths blend into the site where the cottage floats. Simplicity is dominant.

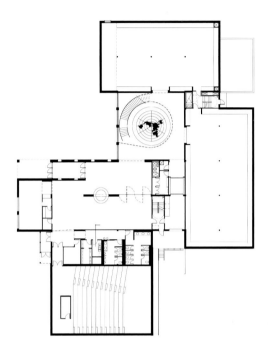

Spurlock Museum
University of Illinois Urbana-Champaign, Urbana-Champaign, Illinois (1996-2000) The new 52,000-square-foot museum is located in a transitional zone between the campus and the community. The museum exhibits 30,000 artifacts from every part of the world. Six galleries were programmed around geographical lines and located in three pavilions or "houses." These houses were arranged around a two-story central core with an additional space for an auditorium. The breakdown of scale and use of masonry, pitched roofs, and ornamental detail provides a collegiate yet residential appearance, which is refreshing in the newly developed campus area.

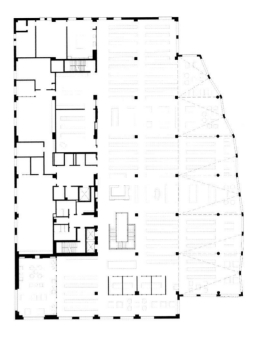

Oak Park Public Library
Oak Park, Illinois

(1995-2003) This 104,000-square-foot, three-story structure with basement parking is located on historic Lake Street with Scoville Park to the east. The Lake Street façade is formal (in stone), reflecting the adjacencies of institutional buildings. The park elevation is informal (glass and copper panels), relating to organic landscape design. The main reading room on the third floor overlooks the park and features a soaring wood ceiling undulating above tree-like wood columns. In the evening, this well-lit space attracts the attention of the community to their public living room.

jazz

Trillium Springs Farmhouse

New Buffalo, Michigan (1993-97) This house is designed for a family of four who live in Chicago as well as Michigan. The site is several hundred acres of fields, which are farmed by the owner. A manmade pond provides the foreground to the south-facing house with heavy woods surrounding the fields. The barn and outbuildings are located at the entry gate beyond.

The building complex is composed of the two-story, three-bedroom main house; a guesthouse with sleeping loft connected by a screen porch; and the garage and farm office connected with a porte cochere/trellis. The L-shaped house is protected by sun screens to the view side with decks and roof terraces which extend the space outdoors. Diagonal views through the first floor expand the visual space. The stone kitchen fire stove and wooden stair anchor the composition.

The screen porch with screen roof provides an outdoor room between the guest quarters and entry. A stone floor here contrasts with the wood floors and decks throughout the rest of the plan. All exterior walls and trellises are natural finish clear cedar siding and trim. Chimney, gutters, and downspouts are lead-coated copper. Black metal is used for window frames, railings, and struts. Interior finishes are laminated pine beams and decking, pine window trim and doors, maple cabinets and furnishings, and mahogany floors. White plaster walls provide a backdrop for this composite of materials.

The idea is a modern Midwest prairie house which is complex in composition but relaxed in attitude. By solving the technical problems of modern structures, the design can solve the functional problems and develop a fresh aesthetic, which complements the environment.

110 Trillium Springs Farmhouse

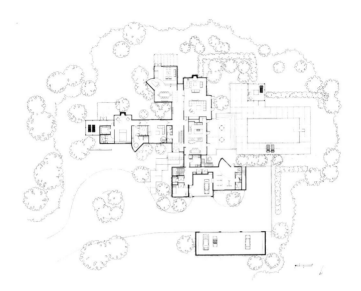

Bannockburn House Bannockburn, Illinois (1994-96)

This house for a family with four children is the most recent exploration of a spiraling or pinwheeling plan with more complex massing and spatial sequences than some of the architect's earlier houses. Because of the large size of the program, it was necessary to break the house into several pavilions to achieve a human scale and more intimate relationships between interior and exterior spaces. The building is not meant to be seen from the exterior in its entirety; rather, it is experienced as a series of episodes or compositions with common themes or motifs recurring throughout. From each aspect it relates to the site in a different way as well, with the disposition of the pavilions forming the north entry court, a pool terrace overlooking a meadow to the west, small private spaces looking into the woods to the east, and roof terraces in each of the three sleeping wings.

Five pavilions spiral around a two-story entry spine, which is set off from the rest of the building in form and material; its curved roof and metal curtainwall contrast with the stucco walls and wood-framed windows of the rest of the house. The main stair is a sculptural piece of brushed stainless steel and glass. The precedent is a modern village and the concept of a complex that integrates function, space, and art.

Highland Park House
Highland Park, Illinois

(1985-86) This house continued the investigation of De Stijl themes explored in earlier houses, but the L-shaped parti, partially determined by the corner lot, became both more complex and more relaxed in plan and section than in earlier projects. Whereas many earlier houses explored spatial and geometric complexity within the confines of a pure geometric form, this plan breaks the box; it is more additive in compositional approach. The interlocking volumes, particularly the stair tower, allow one to move in and out of the dwelling enclosure. These themes were developed further in houses such as the Bannockburn and Dunewood Retreat houses.

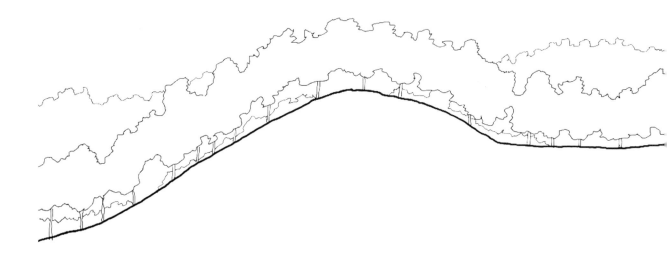

Dunewood Retreat Bridgman, Michigan (1994-1996)

Emphasis on shifting approaches rather than centrality, complete asymmetry, and diagonal views to the outside as well as internal vertical views suggest the syncopated rhythms of jazz. From the entry deck, through the house to the main deck, the spatial flow is linear, but shifting and unpredictable; the overall composition is asymmetrical, breaking the box to form a more complex massing.

In addition to the architect's desire to deal with juxtaposition of forms and spaces, the unusual site and the program contributed to the complexity of the form. The architect designed the family's Chicago house in the University of Chicago neighborhood of Hyde Park in 1980. After living there for over a dozen years, they looked for and found a site for a vacation retreat on a steeply sloping dune in the woods overlooking Lake Michigan. They knew they wanted a very different feel for their second home, accentuating the difference between the urban and country experience. So where the contextual urban house has a more formal arrangement of space and emphasizes front and back on a cubic volume, the country house has a looser arrangement of volumes and a linear form which extends the building into the landscape.

The site posed both a design and construction challenge. The Department of Natural Resources in

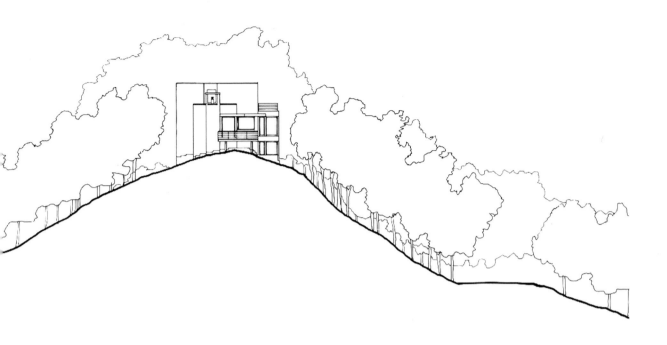

Michigan passed a law stating that no building can be built on a slope greater than 25% within a certain distance of Lake Michigan. On this lot, the only relatively flat land was the top of the dune, a difficult construction site, but one which also afforded the best views. Even the approach was difficult; the drive had to be angled across the hill to achieve a reasonable slope. The contractor built the structure starting at the north end and backed down the site, constructing the garage and stairway last.

The house itself stretches across the hill top 200 feet from garage to living room deck. Horizontal clear cedar siding, metal railings, projecting cedar decks and sunscreens accentuate the linearity of the structure. Lightly stacked screen porches and a roof terrace engage the solid volumes of the three story structure. The main living level at the top of the exterior stairway separates children's rooms below from the parents' above.

From the entry the circulation flows behind the raised family kitchen, under the bridge and into the living room overlooking the lake. The stair to the upper floor acts as a perpendicular counterpoint to the linear organization. The house grows out of its site and visually extends interior space to the outside to create an environment connected to the natural world.

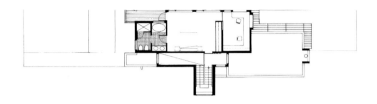

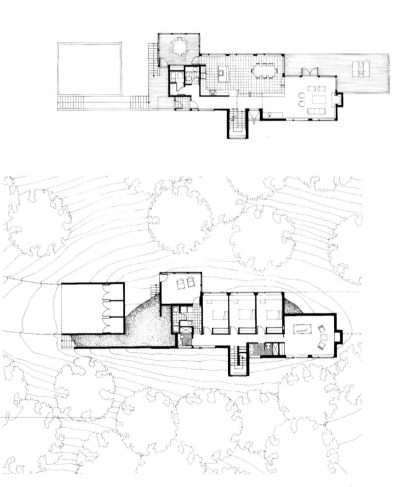

126 Dunewood Retreat

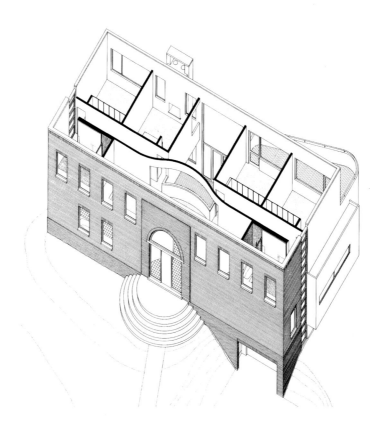

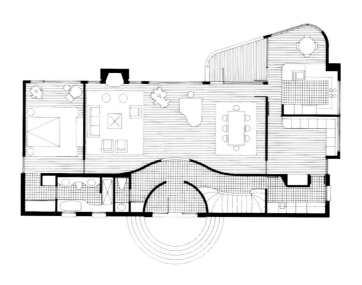

Woodlawn Avenue House

Hyde Park, Chicago (1978-80) This house, designed for the same client as the Dunewood Retreat, is located in the Hyde Park neighborhood on Chicago's south side. It has a formal front façade which relates to the traditional context of Georgian houses on the block, but the relationship between the front and back of the house is not traditional; a more sculptural garden façade in stucco rather than brick suggests that different parts of the structure can respond differently to their immediate contexts, rather than as part of a uniform mass. The overall composition is more formal and more contained than the Dunewood Retreat.

Bridgman House

Bridgman, Michigan (1986-1987) Similar in attitude toward extension of interior space, use of material, and asymmetrical composition, this house, built several years earlier on a similar site nearby, encapsulates many of the ideas of the Dunewood Retreat. Slicing laterally across a wooded sand dune (it was built prior to the 25% slope law), the two-story house is more restrained volumetrically, but also extends interior space to the outside through cantilevered decks which leave the existing dune undisturbed. The second floor open loft space becomes a neutral backdrop from which to contemplate the natural setting.

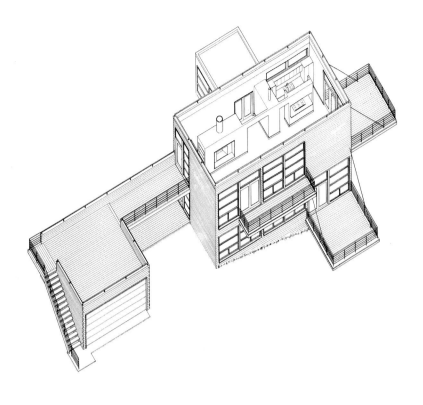

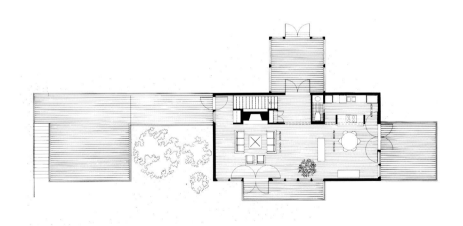

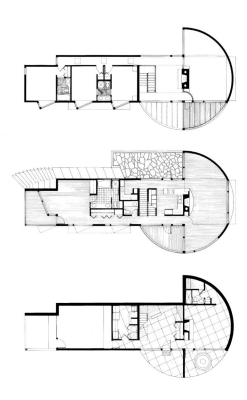

House 1060

Singletree, Colorado (1992-96) The intersection of circle and rectangle form the backdrop for a rhythmic play of projecting elements and negative spaces all related to views and the movement of the sun throughout the year. The gently rolling north slope of the Vail Valley is dry and relatively barren, but there are spectacular mountain views to the south, all of which was taken into account in siting and design.

As in many other houses in this monograph, strong geometry and interior zoning were tightly controlled in plan. In this case, a 16-foot-wide rectangular volume housing private spaces intersects a cylinder with family gathering places, which are symbolized by the central sandstone fireplaces. The narrowness of the house, which is sited perpendicular to the fall line of the hill, kept excavation to a minimum and was easily spanned by engineered plywood joists. Horizontal cedar siding on the rectilinear volume and stucco on the cylinder form a continuous surface on which shadows from the three mountain-facing bays, aluminum sunscreens, and trellises play. Exterior rooms are carved out of the cylinder and screened from the sun.

Hillsborough House Hillsborough, California (1980-82)

This courtyard house with a pool and tennis court was designed as an environment, arranged in a relaxed manner, recalling the California "Bauhaus Modern" of the San Francisco region. Separation of the house into functional wings breaks down its scale and fits it to its hillside site overlooking the San Francisco Bay. A four-foot grid organizes the asymmetrical composition in both plan and elevation, and a glass stair organizes circulation. The entry courtyard off the street provides formal guest approach, while family entry is through the driving court. The language of the house is abstract modern, a stucco and concrete composition with warm interior finishes.

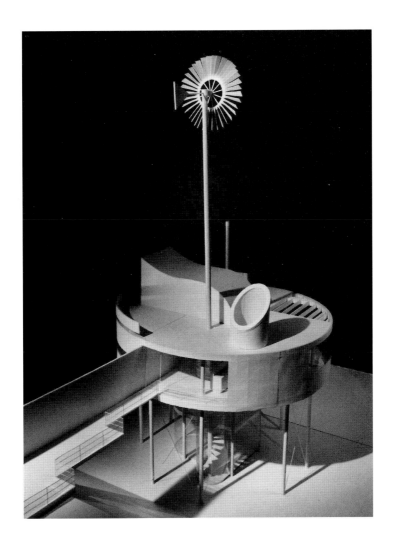

Sundial House
Project (1976) In 1976, seven practicing Chicago architects, calling themselves the Chicago Seven, organized a show of theoretical house designs at the Richard Gray Gallery on Michigan Avenue. The Sundial House was James Nagle's entry. Designed for an abstracted dunes site, the house explores neo-plastic space derived from De Stijl, the forms of Le Corbusier, and the tension between the circle and orthogonal grid. Though it was a theoretical project, it was designed to be buildable, with tight control of form and program within the circle. As Nagle wrote at the time, architecture "should create a harmonic whole and it is best when it achieves a maximum plastic expression while solving the practical requirements."

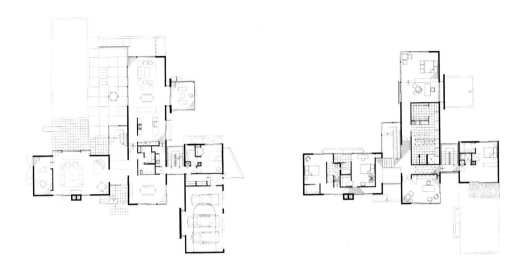

Ravine House
Highland Park, Illinois (1997-2000) The project is an exploration of the conflicting aspects of a structure as shelter and as an integral part of its natural setting. The site fronts on a typical formal suburban street and progresses toward a steeply sloped, wooded ravine. The layering from public to private zones is expressed in the design of the building's exterior envelope. The abstract, detached street façade of stucco and limestone unveils itself with detached planes and an exposed structure to reveal a translucent skin of wood and glass along the ravine edge.

The programmatic layering of public and private zones requires large gathering spaces to be coupled with small intimate sanctuaries. This tension between the manmade and natural, enclosed and integrated, private and public results in a complex form which is more a progression than a singular entity.

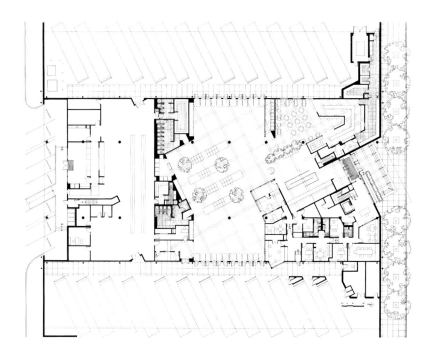

Greyhound Bus Terminal

Chicago, Illinois (1988-1989) A new prototype facility was designed to replace the 35-year-old terminal in Chicago's downtown. The first floor of the new structure is devoted to passenger and parcel arrival and departure. The second floor houses Greyhound's administrative offices which overlook the passenger lounge and are linked by an upper walkway. The required unobstructed canopies span 45 feet over the bus docks, thus the cantinary structure. The interior spaces pick up the bus parking angles and are intended to be a welcoming and active environment in the South Loop.

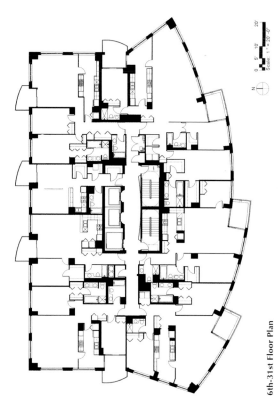

6th-31st Floor Plan

Kinzie Park Tower

Chicago, Illinois (1999-2002) This 34-story, 200-unit high-rise condominium on the Chicago River has a variety of units ranging from studios to three-bedroom suites. Unlike 401 E. Ontario, the units are asymmetrically arranged. The south-facing plans are projected into the city-view space. The north face is straight, defining the Grand Avenue corridor with views to Lake Michigan and the river. The lobby ceiling is flared to reflect the entry façade and natural materials—wood paneling, masonry, and stone—are used to underscore the residential quality of the structure.

Credits

CLASSICS

Translucens House
Dallas, Texas 2004
Project Team NHDKMP Architects Planners Ltd. **Associate Architect** Robert J. Neylan Architects Ltd. **Structural Engineer** Graef, Anhalt, Schloemer & Associates, Ltd. **Mechanical Engineer** WMA Consulting Engineers, Ltd. **General Contractor** Thos. S. Byrne General Contractors **Landscape** Owner/Architect **Client** Withheld at owner's request **Photographer** Scott McDonald © Hedrich Blessing

Dallas House
Dallas, Texas 1973
Project Team James L. Nagle Booth & Nagle Architects **Structural Engineer** Weisinger, Holland **Mechanical Engineer** Wallace-Migdal & Associates, Inc **General Contractor** Wunderlick Construction Co. **Landscape** Owner/Architect **Client** Withheld at owner's request **Photographer** Bill Hedrich © Hedrich Blessing

Architect's Cottage
Door County, Wisconsin 1999
Project Team NHDKM Architects Planners Ltd. **Structural Engineer** Beer, Gorski & Graff, Ltd. **Mechanical Engineer** By Contractor **General Contractor** Leist Construction Co. **Landscape** By Architect with Meissner Landscape **Client** James & Ann Nagle **Photographer** Jim Hedrich © Hedrich Blessing

Carpenter's House
Elmhurst, Illinois 1998
Project Team NHDKM Architects Planners Ltd. **Structural Engineer** Beer, Gorski & Graff, Ltd. **Mechanical Engineer** By Contractor **Interior Design** John Vasilion/Vasilion Associates, Inc. **General Contractor** Joseph Wangler **Landscape** Scott Byron & Company **Client** Withheld at owner's request **Photographer** © Bruce Van Inwegen

Green Lake Cottage
Green Lake, Wisconsin 2003
Project Team NHDKM Architects Planners Ltd. **Structural Engineer** Graef, Anhalt, Schloemer & Associates, Ltd. **Mechanical Engineer** By Contractor **General Contractor** Design Specialty Builders **Landscape** Owner/Architect **Client** Withheld at owner's request **Photographer** © Bruce Van Inwegen

Deerpath House
Door County, Wisconsin 1996
Project Team NHDKM Architects Planners Ltd. **Structural Engineer** Beer, Gorski & Graff, Ltd. **Mechanical Engineer** By Contractor **General Contractor** William Brungraber Construction Company **Landscape** Steve McCarthy with Meissner Landscape **Client** Withheld at owner's request **Photographer** Jim Hedrich © Hedrich Blessing

Durkes House
Dixon, Illinois 1978
Project Team James L. Nagle Booth, Nagle and Hartray Ltd. **Structural Engineer** Beer, Gorski & Graff, Ltd. **Mechanical Engineer** By Contractor **General Contractor** Raymond Harn Construction Company **Landscape** Owner/Architect **Client** Mr. and Mrs. Rick Durkes **Photographer** © Orlando Cabanban

Dunes House

South Haven, Michigan 1991

Project Team Nagle, Hartray & Associates Ltd. **Structural Engineer** Beer, Gorski & Graff, Ltd. **Mechanical Engineer** WMA Consulting Engineers Ltd. **General Contractor** McClanahan Construction Company **Landscape** Nature's Way Landscape **Client** Withheld at owner's request **Photographer** © Hedrich Blessing

Minnesota House

Northern Minnesota 1970

Project Team James L. Nagle Booth & Nagle Architects **Structural Engineer** Weisinger, Holland **Mechanical Engineer** Wallace-Migdal & Associates, Inc. **General Contractor** Arnie Seasted Construction Co. **Landscape** Owner/Architect **Client** Withheld at owner's request **Photographer** © Philip A. Turner

Brown House

Des Moines, Iowa 1970

Project Team James L. Nagle Booth & Nagle Architects **Structural Engineer** Weisinger, Holland **Mechanical Engineer** Wallace-Migdal & Associates, Inc. **General Contractor** Brian Crow Construction Co. **Landscape** Owner/Architect **Client** Dr. & Mrs. William T. Brown **Photographer** © Hedrich Blessing

Lincoln Park House

Chicago, Illinois 1989

Project Team Nagle, Hartray & Associates Ltd. **Structural Engineer** Beer, Gorski & Graff, Ltd. **Mechanical Engineer** WMA Consulting Engineers Ltd. **General Contractor** James A. Blackmore Construction Co. **Landscape** Owner/Architect **Client** Withheld at owner's request **Photographer** © Bruce Van Inwegen © Hedrich Blessing

Evanston House

Evanston, Illinois 1974

Project Team James L. Nagle Booth & Nagle Architects **Structural Engineer** Weisinger, Holland **Mechanical Engineer** Wallace-Migdal & Associates, Inc. **General Contractor** Harold O. Schulz Construction Co. **Landscape** Joe Karr & Associates **Client** Withheld at owner's request **Photographer** © Philip A. Turner

Atrium House

Chicago, Illinois 1988

Project Team Nagle, Hartray and Associates Ltd. **Structural Engineer** Beer, Gorski & Graff, Ltd. **Mechanical Engineer** WMA Consulting Engineers Ltd. **General Contractor** James A. Blackmore Construction Co. **Landscape** Owner **Client** Withheld at owner's request **Photographer** Nagle, Hartray and Associates Ltd.

Hunziker House

Chicago, Illinois 1984

Project Team Nagle, Hartray and Associates Ltd. **Structural Engineer** Beer, Gorski & Graff, Ltd. **Mechanical Engineer** WMA Consulting Engineers Ltd. **General Contractor** James A. Blackmore Construction Co. **Landscape** Joe Karr & Associates **Client** Mr. & Mrs. Robert Hunziker **Photographer** Howard N. Kaplan © HNK Architectural Photography

James Nagle House

Chicago, Illinois 1978

Project Team James L. Nagle Booth, Nagle and Hartray Ltd. **Structural Engineer** Beer, Gorski & Graff, Ltd. **Mechanical Engineer** Wallace-Migdal & Associates, Inc. **General Contractor** Harold O. Schulz Construction Co. **Landscape** Joe Karr & Associates **Client** James & Ann Nagle **Photographer** © Philip A. Turner

Schiller Street Townhouses
Chicago, Illinois 1987
Project Team Nagle, Hartray and Associates Ltd. **Structural Engineer** Beer, Gorski & Graff, Ltd. **Mechanical Engineer** WMA Consulting Engineers, Ltd. **General Contractor** James A. Blackmore Construction Co. **Landscape** By Owner **Client** Mr. Ron Ysla **Photographer** Howard N. Kaplan © HNK Architectural Photography

401 E. Ontario
Chicago, Illinois 1990
Project Team Nagle, Hartray and Associates Ltd. **Structural Engineer** Cohen Barreto Marchertas **Mechanical Engineer** H.S. Nachman & Associates **General Contractor** E.W. Corrigan Construction Company **Landscape** Joe Karr & Associates **Client** Lakeshore Ontario Associates **Photographer** Jim Hedrich © Hedrich Blessing

POPS

Lakeside Retreat
Lakeside, Michigan 1996
Project Team Nagle, Hartray and Associates Ltd. **Structural Engineer** Beer, Gorski & Graff, Ltd. **Mechanical Engineer** WMA Consulting Engineers, Ltd. **General Contractor** Majority Builders **Landscape** Stan Beikmann/Fernwood Landscape **Client** Withheld at owner's request **Photographer** © Bruce Van Inwegen

Hilltop House
Bridgman, Michigan 1989
Project Team Nagle, Hartray and Associates Ltd. **Structural Engineer** Beer, Gorski & Graff, Ltd. **Mechanical Engineer** WMA Consulting Engineers, Ltd. **General Contractor** Design Build, Inc. **Landscape** Owner/Architect **Client** Withheld at owner's request **Photographer** © David Clifton

Shingle House
Union Pier, Michigan 1995
Project Team Nagle, Hartray and Associates Ltd. **Structural Engineer** Beer, Gorski & Graff, Ltd. **Mechanical Engineer** WMA Consulting Engineers, Ltd. **General Contractor** Majority Builders **Landscape** Nature's Way Landscape **Client** Withheld at owner's request **Photographer** © Bruce Van Inwegen

Family Lighthouse
Marshall Point, Wisconsin 1981
Project Team Nagle, Hartray and Associates Ltd. **Structural Engineer** Beer, Gorski & Graff, Ltd. **Mechanical Engineer** Wallace-Migdal & Associates, Inc. **General Contractor** Carlson-Erickson Construction Co. **Landscape** Owner/Architect **Client** Withheld at owner's request **Photographer** Howard N. Kaplan © HNK Architectural Photography

Lakeside House
Lakeside, Michigan 1994
Project Team Nagle, Hartray and Associates Ltd. **Structural Engineer** Beer, Gorski & Graff, Ltd. **Mechanical Engineer** WMA Consulting Engineers, Ltd. **General Contractor**: Majority Builders **Landscape** Owner/Architect **Client** Withheld at owner's request **Photographer** © Hedrich Blessing

Beach House
Door County, Wisconsin 1999
Project Team NHDKM Architects Planners Ltd. **Structural Engineer** Beer, Gorski & Graff, Ltd. **Mechanical Engineer** WMA Consulting Engineers, Ltd. **General Contractor** William Brungraber Construction Company **Landscape** Meissner Landscape **Client** Withheld at owner's request **Photographer** © Bruce Van Inwegen

Spurlock Museum of World Cultures
University of Illinois, Urbana-Champaign 2000
Project Team NHDKM Architects Planners Ltd. **Structural Engineer** TT-CBM Engineers **Mechanical Engineer** WMA Consulting Engineers, Ltd. **General Contractor** Williams Brothers Construction **Client** University of Illinois, Urbana-Champaign **Photographer** © Bruce Van Inwegen

Oak Park Public Library
Oak Park, Illinois 2003
Project Team NHDKMP Architects Ltd. **Structural Engineer** Graef, Anhalt, Schloemer & Associates, Ltd. **Mechanical Engineer** WMA Consulting Engineers, Ltd. **General Contractor** The Meyne Company **Landscape** Carol JH Yetken/CYLA Design Associates, Inc. **Client** Oak Park Public Library **Photographer** Scott McDonald © Hedrich Blessing

JAZZ

Trillium Springs Farmhouse
New Buffalo, Michigan 1997
Project Team NHDKM Architects Planners Ltd. **Structural Engineer** Beer, Gorski & Graff, Ltd. **Mechanical Engineer** WMA Consulting Engineers, Ltd. **General Contractor** Michigan City Builders **Landscape** Maria Smithberg/Artimesa **Client** Withheld at owner's request **Photographer** © Bruce Van Inwegen

Bannockburn House
Bannockburn, Illinois 1996
Project Team NHDKM Architects Planners Ltd. **Structural Engineer** Beer, Gorski & Graff, Ltd. **Mechanical Engineer** By Contractor **Interior Design** Design One, Inc. **General Contractor** Joseph Wangler/Triodyne-Wangler Construction Co., Inc. **Landscape** Scott Byron & Company **Client** Withheld at owner's request **Photographer** © Bruce Van Inwegen

Highland Park House
Highland Park, Illinois 1986
Project Team Nagle, Hartray and Associates Ltd. **Structural Engineer** Beer, Gorski & Graff, Ltd. **Mechanical Engineer** WMA Consulting Engineers, Ltd. **General Contractor** Harold O. Schulz Construction Co. **Client** Withheld at owner's request **Photographer** Howard N. Kaplan © HNK Architectural Photography

Dunewood Retreat
Bridgman, Michigan 1996
Project Team NHDKM Architects Planners Ltd. **Structural Engineer** Beer, Gorski & Graff, Ltd. **Mechanical Engineer** WMA Consulting Engineers, Ltd. **General Contractor** Michigan City Builders **Landscape** Nature's Way Landscape **Client** Withheld at owner's request **Photographer**: © Bruce Van Inwegen

Woodlawn Avenue House
Chicago, Illinois 1980
Project Team Nagle, Hartray and Associates Ltd. **Structural Engineer** Beer, Gorski & Graff, Ltd. **Mechanical Engineer** WMA Consulting Engineers, Ltd. **General Contractor** Schultz & Blackmore Construction Co. **Landscape** Joe Karr & Associates **Client** Withheld at owner's request **Photographer** © Hedrich Blessing

Bridgman House
Bridgman, Michigan 1987
Project Team Nagle, Hartray and Associates Ltd. **Structural Engineer** Beer, Gorski & Graff, Ltd. **Mechanical Engineer** WMA Consulting Engineers, Ltd. **General Contractor** Carrol Ott Construction Co. **Landscape** Nature's Way **Client** Withheld at owner's request **Photographer** © Hedrich Blessing

House 1060
Singletree, Colorado 1996

Project Team Nagle, Hartray and Associates Ltd. **Structural Engineer** Beer, Gorski & Graff, Ltd. **Mechanical Engineer** WMA Consulting Engineers, Ltd. **General Contractor** Wydeveld Construction Co. **Landscape** Owner/Architect **Client** Withheld at owner's request **Photographer** © David Clifton

Hillsborough House
Hillsborough, California 1982

Project Team Nagle, Hartray and Associates Ltd. **Structural Engineer** Beer, Gorski & Graff, Ltd. **Mechanical Engineer** WMA Consulting Engineers, Ltd. **General Contractor** Del Large Construction Co. and Owner **Landscape** Peter Calender Landscape **Client** Withheld at owner's request **Photographer** © Hedrich Blessing

Sundial House
Theoretical Project, 1976

Project Team James L. Nagle **Photographer** © Orlando Cabanban

Ravine House
Highland Park, Illinois 2000

Project Team NHDKM Architects Planners Ltd. **Structural Engineer** Beer, Gorski & Graff, Ltd. **Mechanical Engineer** By Contractor **Interior Design** Cannon/Frank **General Contractor** Joseph Wangler/Triodyne-Wangler Construction Co., Inc. **Landscape** Scott Byron & Company **Client** Withheld at owner's request **Photographer** © Bruce Van Inwegen

Greyhound Bus Terminal
Chicago, Illinois 1989

Project Team Nagle, Hartray and Associates Ltd. **Structural Engineer** Cohen-Barreto-Marchertas **Mechanical Engineer** Wallace-Migdal & Associates, Inc. **General Contractor** W.E. O'Neil Construction Co. **Landscape** Joe Karr & Associates **Client** Greyhound Lines **Photographer** © Hedrich Blessing

Kinzie Park Tower
Chicago, Illinois 2001

Project Team NHDKM Architects Planners Ltd. **Structural Engineer** Chris P. Stefanos, Inc. **Mechanical Engineer** GKC/EME, LLC **General Contractor** E.W. Corrigan Construction Co. **Landscape** Joe Karr & Associates **Client** The Habitat Company **Photographer** Jim Hedrich © Hedrich Blessing

Acknowledgements

The first credit goes to the wonderful clients we have had the pleasure of collaborating with through the building process. They have supported our work and several have commissioned additions to the homes we designed and other new projects. We also have a nice history of working with repeat contracting firms who are very important to a successful product.

Thanks especially to Kristin Baker in our office who "put the book together" with talent and enthusiasm. And thanks to Stanley Tigerman for his long support, and Kathleen Nagle who began the logbook.

The partnership makes the practice work. Jack Hartray's technical expertise and humor are essential. Dirk Danker, Howard Kagan, Don McKay, and Eric Penney design and produce the firm's projects. The Oak Park Public Library, Spurlock Museum, Kinzie Park Tower, and many new undertakings, including residences, are examples of a good future.

Our associates, Bill Duke, John Gleichman, and Michelle Sakayan, along with Julianne Scherer, Tim Sheridan, and others, have all worked on the buildings produced here.

At the risk of missing some, we want to include the following talented architects who have (in order of the buildings presented here) been instrumental in each project's completion. They include: Robert Neylan, William Montebano, Chris Rudolph, Jerry Walleck, Doo Ho Lee, Mary Patera, Alexander Hartray, William Sitton, Robert Lubowsky, Gint Lietuvninkas, Marvin Ullman, Charles Grund, Charles Riesterer, David Jennerjahn, James Highum, Ericka Pagel, Patrick Jones, McShane Murnane, Joanne Connelly, Michael Messerle, Julie Deprey, Howard Decker, Carl Gergits, Jeffrey Straesser, Fernando Fen, Clara Wineberg, Chris Foley, Chris Lanzisera, and we're sure several more.

- Jim Nagle